The College of Mental Health Counselling presents:

Evaluations of an Online Counsellor Training Course

STUDENT COMMENTS AND EVALUATIONS

Daniel Keeran, MSW, President
www.ctihalifax.com

ISBN-13: 978-1535385619

ISBN-10: 1535385618

Printed in the United States of America.

Dedicated to the Quest for Inner Healing

Mental Health Counsellor Training Course

www.ctihalifax.com

for the

Certificate of Mental Health Counselling and Therapy

STUDENT COMMENTS AND EVALUATIONS

Canada: Ontario, Alberta, British Columbia, Nova Scotia, Newfoundland, Saskatchewan, New Brunswick, Yukon Territory

United States, Australia, Thailand, Trinidad and Tobago, China, India, Africa

Wendy T., North Vancouver, BC

I have no previous education in counseling and thought that the many books on psychology and self-help topics gave me sufficient insight to be a successful counselor, but having done this course I realize that I had not even begun to understand the art of good counseling. I think that **the knowledge attained from this course is incredible**. I am so **thrilled to have the book both electronically and in paperback** to use as a textbook for reference and will continue to read it many, many more times.

I work as a Special Needs assistant and have found that I **have already used many of these newly acquired skills** both in the school environment as well as in my ministry with women. I would like to understand more about how to become a professional counselor and then make a decision as to whether to proceed with this as a career or to continue to use it in my existing environments. I have never been to a counseling session personally so **this was absolutely incredible value** and I have no doubt that if I were to implement **these incredibly practical steps and techniques** that I could be a very effective counselor. I certainly would never have guessed that **wording would be**

so important to the process. Daniel, I love that your heart is to help people become healthy. May you be blessed as you bless others.

Diane S., Alberta

The text for the course is an exceptional resource.

My copy is now worn looking and I have read it a minimum of 5 to 6 times. I think the course has provided the knowledge and skills necessary for a solid foundation for counseling people seeking help.

The text provides a good foundation or counseling. It is clearly and practically written, so easy to understand. Examples throughout assist the student in visioning using the strategies and are of course, very interesting.

Amanda S., Ontario

I found the course to be **very informative and helpful with practical approaches** shared for better understanding on how to actually move forward with the information learned. I am already a Child and Youth Counselor, but I feel that this course elaborated on techniques and introduced new learning for me, especially where there are differences with adult/couple counseling compared to child/youth counseling. I feel I have **a solid foundation for counseling people of all ages** now.

I found that the text was a very useful resource and I know that I will continue to use it. I am **looking forward to re-reading it**, to gain more insight, without the pressures of answering questions.

The text provided skills, knowledge an experiences that I wanted to acquire to further my professional development as a counselor. I really found the examples of what to say with specific clients in specific situations to be helpful.

I would recommend this course to others who are interested in becoming professional counsellors because I feel it is **well laid out**, with a great text resource to refer to. It allowed sufficient time (with extensions if needed), which I found helpful, as I was recently called back to work full time, I am a single mom, and I have a house to take care of multiple part time jobs.

When I initially registered for the course, I was laid off of my job and only working part time hours, with kids in school. I thought this would be a good time to do the course. Things changed and it became a bit more difficult to find the needed time. I enjoyed the program, so that made it easier to try to find the necessary time.

I believe the cost was reasonable for the course content and resources. I was impressed at the speedy delivery of the text and the **quick response to my emails**. It was very much appreciated.

I definitely received value in counseling skills and knowledge by completing this course.

Darlene S., Nova Scotia

I have recommended this program to several people and feel it **should become a mandatory course** for all health care and service providers. Very in-depth and effective yet easy to follow and line upon line teaching.

Anna S., High River, Alberta

I enjoyed this course as it **made me aware of areas of personal development** and communication that I personally could grow and how I could help or facilitate others to grow. This very practical course gave me a **lot of new sentences or phrases** that I have never thought of using before. I have found that trust and **confidence of a client really increases if I am fluent or "word perfect" in my approach**.

The **text was clear and understandable**, especially for me who practice English as a fourth Language.

I have found **this course in particular to address a wide variety of issues**, especially the most common in the community. I would

recommend this course especially because it gives **so many practical examples** of how to address specific issues. It **equips a counsellor** to present themselves skilled and professional.

Signe K., Winnipeg, Manitoba

This course really **helped me to examine my own mental health** and how it affects my relationships. It also helped me **to evaluate healthy versus unhealthy patterns** and coping mechanisms in myself and others. One reason I took this course was that I often find people opening up to me when we are talking and I wanted to be able to respond in appropriate and helpful way rather than leading them or just compounding their emotions. This **course has met my expectations** in this way as I have had multiple opportunities to practice the counselling skills in everyday conversation.

I feel **better equipped to help people** who seek me out for help with words and phrases that clearly help the person come to their own understanding of their issues, rather than just offering advice or commiserating with them. I have also felt **better equipped to talk assertively** with my ex-partner and have a clearer way of expressing my feelings and not feeling guilty for my opinions.

The **text is clear, and written in a conversational, familiar style** indicates the relaxed attitude the counsellor can use in communication with clients. It is somewhat repetitive, but as the same or similar prompts and responses are useful in multiple situations, I found this appropriate.

I am happy with the knowledge and skills I have learned from this course and am certain that I have gotten great value for the tuition. The course materials have been **beneficial in both my personal and professional relationships**.

Anita H., London, Ontario

I found the course gave me more **insight into my own experiences** with grief and loss which I was not expecting. It exceeded my expectations with regards to giving me more knowledge on **how to speak with my clients** on a personal but professional basis in order to help them with their problems.

I believe this course has helped provide me with a base of knowledge that will **help me in assessing the issues** my clients bring to me in order to help them heal. The text book was clear and understandable, and contained **many examples** of real world experiences. I look forward to using the skills I have acquired in helping my clients understand and heal from the issues in their past which have caused them to self-harm.

I would **definitely recommend this course** to others wanting to become counsellors. I think the **value of this course exceeds what you actually invest** into it.

Susan W., Yukon Territory

This course has exceeded my expectations and has certainly has given me a solid foundation. I am so very grateful for this course it will help me in my work. Oh yes, the book and the exam were written well.

I work in a **women's shelter**, and two of my coworkers are taking the course. I recommended the course if one does want to counsel. I really think this was a good deal, because I learned a lot more than the cost of tuition.

Aaron W., Missouri

The course greatly exceeded my expectations! It was reasonably priced and I learned a lot more than I thought I was going to. **I learned just as much or more than I would have if I went to a University**.

What I learned from this course has given me a great foundation and deeper insight into the counseling process and I am confident in my abilities to help people seeking counseling.

The text was very well written and it was very understandable. It prepared me well for the qualifying exam and my future in professional counseling.

I would definitely recommend this course to others who are interested in becoming professional counsellors. The value of counseling skills and knowledge I gained from this course greatly exceeded the cost of tuition!!

Kristina S.P., Ontario

After developing and initiating a Suboxone therapy program for clients with opioid addiction, it became apparent that mental health counselling and therapy skills were essential to a nurse practicing in this field. After researching and reviewing various educational modalities to compliment my practice, I felt the Mental Health Counselling and Therapy certificate course with The College of Mental Health to best fit my needs. **The course outline provided exposure to all the required content to be utilized to optimally treat the clients I serve**.

The course material was delivered in a manner conducive to a working professional, with content and lessons easy to navigate and complete. Course material was **relevant to current day practice**, and conveyed in an organic integrated format.

Upon achieving completion of this course, I am able to better understand mental illness with the use various therapeutic interventions. Reflecting on this program's educational pathway, I am confident to advocate for the use of this course as **part of the curriculum of all nursing programs**.

With the completion of this course I have now expanded my professional portfolio and since been **offered a position with the Addiction Centre as the Regional Manager**. I sincerely recommend this course to anyone working with clients suffering any form of mental illness. It was **well worth the cost** of the tuition.

Catherine S., New Brunswick

This course was **much more than I thought it would be in terms of content**. The **assignments were very helpful** in that research from other sources was required as well.

Various **situations were covered and what to say and how to say it** were laid out nicely in the textbook. The topics were presented in an organized format and the **text was very easy to follow**.

I took this course to further my skill in dealing with the intake portion of my Reiki sound therapy practice. Also at the end of a session clients will discuss aspects of their lives that **I now feel more equipped** dealing with.

This **course is extremely comprehensive**. There is information which is presented that is **not found in other types of similar courses**.

In my sincere opinion I **absolutely received value in counseling skills and knowledge exceeding the cost of tuition** for this course.

Beth L., Lansdowne, Ontario

This course has definitely met my expectations by giving me concrete tools, **words to say to illicit the best response**, and by confirming what I believed to be true regarding unresolved grief and loss issues. **I have both a college and a university degree** but I wanted specific training on doing grief work and this course exceeded my expectations in that department.

I also like that Professor Keeran has written this book as a way to empower counsellors and the general public to help create a healthier society.

The Assessment is a good template and intake process from which to base the clients counselling goals on. The counsellor responses are all **simple yet powerful** if used correctly. The text builds on my already sound knowledge of solution focused therapy.

The text is obviously written from the experience of someone who has years of successful practice doing this work. The text was easy to read and understand **without the usual psychology "babble speak" found in most college and university texts**.

The scenarios are all more real life than "hypothetical," and I have found the **strategies more helpful than much of what I learned in my college training** in social services. Professor Keeran has mastered the art of "keeping it simple."

I believe that Professor Keeran has provided **all the essential skills and responses for helping clients move through their pain** and onto a path of health and wellness. The rest I believe will come with time and practice.

There are many counsellors who would not be willing to **share their counselling "secrets."** Professor Keeran has done a beautiful thing by **sharing his tried, tested and true best practices** found in many years of counselling experience.

I **definitely feel like I received a good value** for the money I paid for this course. I paid $20,000 for a university degree that was valuable in its own right, but this is **giving me more tangible skills than my degree**. What I was looking for was more training to add to my college diploma and university degree that would give me the confidence and skills needed to become a grief counsellor in private practice. While I could have done that with the education I already had, **I didn't feel qualified to do so. Now I do.**

UPDATE: Got the job! Just wanted to let you know that I was offered and accepted a part-time therapist position with CTAT in Kingston. I started my training on Friday and am being groomed to work with ritual abuse survivors. I will also be able to focus on grief work and the centre has offered to allow me to run my private grief therapy practice through the centre when I am ready to get it up and running. How amazing is that? I am so happy that I took your course because it has opened some wonderful doors for me. Thank you.

Nicole B., Waterloo, Ontario

In my most sincere opinion, **the course definitely met and exceeded**

my expectations. The knowledge I have received in this course has built a **solid foundation** for my future in a **counselling career**; when I read other counselling material it will make sense and have a place.

The **text was very practical** and useful; I believe it **truly MADE** the course. I want to develop skills in crisis counselling and in child and youth counselling. In fact I may take your specialized courses later on. I would **recommend this course to others** because it was very straightforward, and straight to the point. **Each paragraph** in the text is useful and **each chapter** is applicable.

Amanda M., Fort Frances, Ontario

This course has **exceeded my expectations**. It has given me the knowledge, skills and judgement to help clients who are struggling with hardships. I feel a lot more comfortable asking certain questions to clients now as well as carrying on a conversation with individuals.

The knowledge and skills that I have learned from this course has given me a **strong foundation for counselling** individuals who are seeking help. It has given me the process to follow when doing a clinical assessment on clients. It has also given me communication skills.

I **found the text amazing**. All questions I had before starting this course were found in the text. I feel through this course I have **learned so much about myself** and the skills I need to be able to be a counsellor to help others that are dealing with such hardships. This course has made me want to further my education in the counselling world.

I would **recommend this course to others who are interested in becoming professional counsellors** because it gives you the ground on where to start with counselling. It teaches you the proper ways to start a session, continue through the session and close the session.

In my opinion the knowledge and counselling skills I have received from this program is going to help me greatly in my field of work. This program has **exceeded all my expectations**, and I look forward to helping individuals within my community using the guides I have learned from this course.

Tony T., Norwood, Ontario

My **expectations have definitely been exceeded**. I was not expecting this much immediately applicable information in the course. The theoretical skills have been covered in a way that will allow me to **start using them immediately**.

As a teacher at an acupuncture college, I think that acquiring counselling skills will help acupuncture graduates be of more help to their patients. The **value I received in counselling skills and knowledge** *absolutely* **exceeded the cost of tuition** for this course.

Joseph C., Holstein, Ontario

I believe that the knowledge and skills I received from this course are **worthy of much higher tuition**. I further feel very strongly that this course provides the same skills as other programs which take longer and charge standard college or University prices.

Lorrie G., Cambridge, Ontario

The course content exceeded my expectation. It covers most of the cases that will be seen and allows for a good knowledge base. I believe the knowledge and skills learned in this course will definitely **give me a great foundation for counselling. Very in-depth!!**

The text was very easy to understand. I would **recommend this course to anyone** who is interested in this field; even seasoned counsellors would find this course to be a great refresher.

Danny N., Pickering, Ontario

This course was **very insightful and educational**. It did meet my expectations of acquiring the fundamental knowledge of effective counseling skills. I now am more aware of what reflective statements and validating statements are, different types of interventions involved, how to conduct a counselling session and important ethical and relationship boundaries. The **text was written in a very clear and understandable way**. It provided many examples of different situations and counselling sessions.

I have **already used some of the techniques I have learned in this course with my family**. Everyone has conflicts, losses and unresolved or unfinished business. This is a good starting point in understanding how to deal with those losses and unfinished businesses. Also it helps knowing how to be an assertive individual and have effective communication skills to pass on to your family as well as using it to deal with people you interact with on a day to day basis.

This **course provides many examples of using clear and effective communication and conflict resolution skills** and allows the counsellor to have a list of appropriate **reflecting and validating statements**.

Lori K., Counsellor, Ottawa, Ontario

The **book was great and definitely exceeded my expectations**. I feel the course has made me feel **confident in my skills**. I enjoyed the text and I felt it was laid out in an easy manner to learn. I would recommend this course to others who are interested in becoming professional counsellors. The course was comprehensive and I **definitely feel it was worth what I paid**.

William A., Mississauga, Ontario

Looking forward to pursuing a career in mental health counseling, I believe that **the course, based on the book's contents, has covered all issues that one could encounter in practice**. It has **exceeded my expectations**.

It has set up clear guidelines and provided simple well-phrased statements and questions that cover all aspects in counseling. I feel confident that what I have learned so far has given me a solid foundation for professional counseling. The **text was very clear and understandable** and was presented in a simple language which I think is the same language a counselor would use in practice.

Dorothy M., Jarvie, Alberta

The content **exceeded my expectations**. It taught me to think "outside the box." The **simple language** teaches it is important to learn something new every day, which makes the student a better future counsellor. With continual referral to the book, I will be ensured my counselling techniques are conducted a sincere way.

The **text was devoted to simple language**. The book teaches you to be honest and straightforward with clients. I am a retired police officer, so this course was important, as I have **plans to start a badly needed N.A. program and do peer counselling** in the community.

This course has **taught me more of the necessary tools to work on myself**, be more aware of my behaviours and patterns.

I would **recommend the program to anyone dedicated to the counselling world and the people that need the help**. The student has to be willing to dedicate time, energy and have a serious desire to learn. This course was a well-balanced learning tool.

Velna B., Ft. McMurray, Alberta

The course has **definitely more than met my expectations**. The material was very clear, practical, and easy for me to understand. This course has given me a wealth of knowledge and skills to help me in counseling people.

The knowledge about the family of origin and where it all begins for a person was like common knowledge for me, but the book reinforced that even more and sure **let me see personally why we think and do the things we do**.

I feel like the book **covered everything you would need to know in order to do counseling**. It will be a book that I'll **always refer to for life** while doing counseling. I am very grateful for having the opportunity to do this course. It has helped me considerably in every way.

The course has helped me personally to understand feelings and deal with issues in my own life. I quote the book as saying: "a counselor in training that is not willing to engage and accept his own pain and to integrate the parts of himself, may not believe in the importance of his client doing that." This course have **given me more confidence**, and made me more confident when talking to people concerning their needs.

The **text was written in a very clear and understandable way** and it provided useful, essential skills and details for becoming a successful professional counsellor. The book has great essential skills and details to help people through life's conflicts and losses.

I would highly **recommend this course and already have recommended it** because I believe it's a great foundational course for anyone who is interested in professional counseling. This is a great course to keep building on. I know the course can benefit you personally as well as learning how to help someone else.

Sarah C., Calgary, Alberta

I have **already begun incorporating many of the skills and techniques from this course into my work as a Crisis Line Counsellor**, particularly the use of the suicide contract. Prior to this course I did not see the benefit of looking too deeply at the family of origin and the parent's communication styles however, I am now finding it is very useful in helping clients/callers understand their triggers and defenses and gain insight into their current dysfunctional behaviours.

The main benefit I received from taking this course was the flexibility it offered. I was able to study and work through the assignments at my own pace and when I had time. I very much **appreciated receiving prompt answers to my questions** from Daniel. The techniques introduced in the book were easy to follow, and the terms used were adequately explained for ease of understanding.

I would **recommend this course to anyone wanting to acquire essential counselling skills for application in a practical setting**, particularly to those students who are currently studying psychology. I would also **recommend the text to anyone who is considering going into therapy themselves or is recommending counselling to a loved one** and would like to gain a better understanding of what to expect when entering into a counselling relationship with a therapist.

Megan P., Alberta

This course exceeded my expectations with the thoroughness of the textbook, and the depth of the exam was intense, but after completing it, I feel even more assured in my counselling abilities.

Since enrolling in the course I have already found myself **listening to my friends' "problems" in a different way**. Before the course I always used to have suggestions for what was wrong in the current situation, but after reading the text and completing the assignments, I have learned that these problems could be recurring issues or unresolved conflicts from the past. I think this especially will help me dig deeper in my counselling sessions to find underlying meanings of different issues.

I found the **textbook very enjoyable**. I found it especially helpful that Mr. Keeran provided so many first-hand accounts. I thought that this textbook provided the fundamental building blocks to becoming a skilled counsellor.

I have **already referred a friend to enrol in this course**. I did so because I found the course to be very flexible with my schedule. I found the textbook to be an enjoyable read, and I **particularly enjoyed completing the Clinical Assessment on myself**. I found that assignment to be essential in my personal and professional development as a counsellor.

UPDATE: M.P. was offered a counselling position in a local family and social services agency shortly after completing the initial course. Then after one year she was offered a position in a local hospice program.

Larry M., Alberta

I was apprehensive that I would learn to professionally counsel somebody effectively without any other previous training. I was definitely wrong. The textbook was packed with all the information that I would need. I learned the clinical assessment, numerous interventions, conduct expectations and ethics, and got an inside look at the counselling profession by hearing about first hand experiences. The **question and answer assignment was brilliant**. By making up questions I got to know what was truly important surrounding the counselling assessment, session, and relationship. This course **exceeded my expectations by far**.

This course has given me a **solid foundation for counselling people** who are seeking help. I have the knowledge of personality types, common mental health disorders, and defenses that I will need to work with. I have the skills to teach problem-solving skills to couples as well as a one-on-one client. This course has given me the knowledge of the importance of client-lead counselling. This is crucial to a client's self-awareness and if not done properly does not benefit the client at all.

When first reading the text I was nervous about remembering everything that I was reading. The more I read the more it made sense and linked all together. I liked how it took you step by step into the situations that you may encounter.

It was **quite incredible how I would pause to ask a question, to have it answered only a few sentences later**. While writing the exam I found the **text an excellent reference guide and it was easy to remember** exactly where I had read something. The text also clearly outlines interventions like the gestalt awareness and empty chair exercises. It is a book that I will continuously go back to in my career.

I have already looked into the continuing studies courses provided with the college and are excited to gain more knowledge in certain areas such as adult survivors of childhood abuse. I am hoping to volunteer at a local woman's shelter to gain experience with counselling.

I would **highly recommend this course to others** who are interested in becoming professional counsellors. I am a very hands-on learner so I really enjoyed the assignment of making questions and then answering them. It got me to look at what was really important. I enjoyed the practice clinical assessment with a volunteer. It built my confidence in knowing that this is definitely something I could see myself doing. I could already see the relevance of what I had learned and what I was hearing from the volunteer.

This course allowed me to do some more **work on myself** in preparation for helping others. A lot of knowledge could be applied to my own life patterns and made become more aware of my own behavior. I feel like I have a great foundation of necessary knowledge and skills. I am left feeling confident that I can successfully counsel someone and help them live a happier life.

The structure of the course was perfect for my lifestyle. I am a very busy Mom of a toddler and work full-time. I was able to do all of the work during nap time and after he went to bed. If you are motivated, you will have no problem getting this course done because you get to set the hours at which you study.

I would **definitely recommend this course** to someone who has been out of the classroom for a while and is very independent and motivated.

Dylan L., Alberta

The course **exceeded my expectations in that it was more intense than I expected**. However, it was very insightful and informative. It covered counselling in a way that was easy to read and understand. I found it very beneficial to me. I believe the **skills I learned in the course are basic,**

essential and effective for developing a therapeutic relationship with a solid foundation for counselling people.

In my opinion the text was **written in a clear understandable way, for providing useful, essential skills and details for becoming a successful professional counsellor**. If I were to develop further as a professional counsellor I feel I have acquired the kinds of skills, knowledge and experiences to further my development.

I would **recommend this course to others who are interested in becoming a professional counsellor** because it gives you the kinds of skills, knowledge and experiences that you need to become a professional counsellor. It's the 'bible' for professional counselling.

Gary P., Alberta

The course has **exceeded my expectations in that I was expecting to learn different techniques and interventions**. However, I was not expecting there to be such a focus on proper wording and statements, and I see how this is imperative to the counselling process.

The knowledge and skills learned has **given me a solid foundation for counselling people who are seeking help by giving practical methods** of connecting people with their feeling and relating their current issues to their past. I think the practical wording of statements given throughout the text was very helpful in providing how to effectively communicate with clients.

The **text was written in a very practical way and the essential skills and interventions were well written** and laid out in a way that was not too complex to grasp.

To further my development I am interested in learning how to communicate and pass on very practical tools that will help clients in their issues. I can see myself as more of an encourager and a coach.

I would **recommend this course to others as it is written in very practical terms**. I found that the counsellor response exam was very useful in being able to apply the different wording and therapeutic statements and interventions that were taught throughout the book.

Robert R., Alberta

This course has **exceeded my expectations**. It has taught me **many useful techniques and methods of counselling** individuals, and I have been enlightened in many ways as a professional counsellor.

There is more to counselling than simply listening to a client talk about emotional issues; a counsellor must be able to demonstrate a wide variety of skills. These include **empathy, compassion, understanding, challenging skills, motivational ability, creative thinking** and much more. A counsellor must also be able to listen to a client's problems and concerns and translate these into goals that the client can work towards in order to reach resolution. This course has **provided me with additional skills and it has increased my knowledge significantly**.

The **text was written in a clear and understandable way**. It taught me a variety of subjects such as respect and dignity for all clients. It showed ways of dealing with supporting and alleviating distress. I appreciated the information about the differences in culture and human experience, and the importance of remaining non-judgmental. It taught me how to adequately provide counselling services and to maintain client confidentiality and ethical principles.

The kinds of skills, knowledge, and experiences that I want to acquire are: the ability to assist individuals with the process of being freed from negative emotional distress and mental confusion; to provide the opportunity for clients to gain control of their fears and manage the issues which are causing adverse stress in their life; to guide the individual to make positive changes that they desire to experience in their life; the ability to skillfully encourage and support the client throughout the course of their healing journey.

I would **recommend this course to others** who are interested in becoming professional counsellors mainly because I believe it provides a well-balanced and thorough counselling program. It is very informative, and it helps the counsellor to better understand the client. It provides practical pointers in a non-complicated manner. It teaches a variety of ways how to deal with various scenarios one will encounter in their counselling ministry.

Terry P., Alberta

This course has **exceeded my expectations by far**. I did not expect to complete the course and be ready to begin counselling. However, I believe that I have been given the foundation and fundamentals for a future counselling career.

This course has provided an insight into the ultimate goals of the counselling relationship, the background for various types of issues and concerns that people are facing, and the skills to assist them in working through the **process of identifying their personal issues and moving beyond them into new healthy behaviours**.

The text was very clear and easy to read. **Of all the courses that I have completed, it was no doubt the most clear and comprehensive and useful that I have ever experienced.**

I would **definitely recommend this course to others** who are interested in becoming professional counsellors.

Thomas J., Alberta

This **course has been a God-send for me**. I have been dealing with my own feeling of grief and loss, and this course has helped me to make sense of it all, all my emotions and feelings. All of my thoughts any why I feel the way I do. It has also helped me to avoid making unhealthy patterns and decisions. So thank you.

I have found that I learned that **behind every action, there's a reason** for it. We all have our crosses to bear; it's how we deal with them that gets us up and going again. I want more than anything to take my own life experiences and the knowledge this course has given me to help people move past their grief and into all that life has to offer, to make a difference in this world, to leave a mark.

Considering this was my first counselling course, I did find some of the wording to kind of go over my head little. But the more I got into the book the more terms I understood. And the **references in the back of the book were a tremendous help. I also liked how the exam was laid out** and not all over the book. There was a pattern to it all which I found made it much easier.

This **course has laid the foundation** for me to continue my education and become a social worker. This has given me the boost I needed!!! I would **recommend this to ANYONE wishing to become a counsellor** because it covers such a broad range of issues and allows you to understand why people act and react the way they do. It gives you a great knowledge to build upon.

Harold L., Professional Counsellor, Alberta

I have a Master's Degree in religion, concentration in Christian Counselling. I am the Counselling Pastor at FCC. Besides offering professional counselling services, **my role is to develop, implement and administer a counselling program** for the church.

We envision a counselling centre offering counselling services to the faith community and the community at large. I would love for my leadership team to do your course. Of all my studies, the one I found the most helpful and useful to this day was *Effective Counselling Skills* by Daniel Keeran, MSW (President of the College).

UPDATE: H.L. enrolled nine individuals in the program and is preparing to provide much-needed counselling services to the community where he lives.

Sandra D., Mission, British Columbia

The knowledge and skills I've learned so far will help by grounding me and allow me to **continue to be grounded by referring back to the content of the course**. The text is clear, concise, explanatory and insightful.

This course is unique in that Daniel's idea of **understanding one's own issues before dealing with other's issues** is brilliant. There are different ways of using the information and insight in this course is so diverse in that way.

In my sincere opinion, I believe I **got more out of this than I thought I would**. Daniel's **immediate and continued support is wonderful**. I will **recommend the course text be read by any and all who have a thirst for knowledge, about themselves and insight into others**.

Krysty M., Vancouver Island, British Columbia

Being able to take the **course online suited my needs** very well. The price was more than adequate and suited to my financial situation. The payment plan was sufficient and easy to follow through on.

I feel I developed an **awareness of letting the client guide sessions**. I realized how important it is **not to project my own hopes** or other personal feelings onto the client. There were **ways introduced to me to ask important questions** of the client without being aggressive.

The **information the text book provided in of itself was incredible** and I loved the assessment set up, explanation of theories and philosophies of the author, as well as the verbal questions one would ask during a session.

The **low cost and great insights provided in the text would be great reasons to recommend this course** to others. This is a **good precursor to entering into the field of counselling**. I **gained a level of**

professionalism, policy and protocol that has previously been lacking in my personal home business of life coaching.

Steven R., Chilliwack, British Columbia

I **wouldn't hesitate to recommend this course to anyone** – even if it's for personal growth.

This course has **exceeded my expectations** because the content is so valuable. I didn't expect the actual qualifying examination to be so long… LOL! I'm also glad that it was **so thorough and detailed**. I need to know the content, and the questions helped me to absorb the information. I also enjoyed and was **challenged by the open book format** because it forced me to seek out the answers when I wasn't sure and then I read more material as I did so.

I've been an organiser and facilitator for various support style groups for many years – This course has given me **more knowledge of mental health issues** and also a better understanding of **how to say things** and "what" to say to people in specific situations.

I felt that the **text was extremely clear** and was written in a way that seemed to provide me with **the "meat and potatoes" of counselling** terms, techniques and the process needed to be effective. I really enjoyed the over-all presentation; especially how thorough it is considering it is done at home.

I need to have a working understanding of the appropriate things to say at specific times and during certain circumstances during counselling. For example, **what to say when a client misses an appointment and if they disclose abuse, etc… Very helpful!**

For the benefit of the knowledge alone, I received great value. I would say the **tuition is very low and the value is extremely high**. I am going to purchase the other book and sign up for more courses soon.

I have a passion for facilitating support groups and am the facilitator, trainer and leader for the weekly mood disorder groups, addiction support groups and marriage mentoring groups in my community. It is a real blessing.

UPDATE: I just finished my first week in my new career at a local Christian mission in the residential treatment centre department as a residential site supervisor. This is a great opportunity for me and has enabled me to be in a position for many great future opportunities. This has been made possible thanks to my training and continuing experience with the College of Mental Health Counselling-I am so very greatful for this. I also will continue to see clients privately.

June 6, 2014 - Just wanted to let you know that I got a really good career move today with a promotion to men's program manager at a treatment centre in Chilliwack. This is an excellent promotion - I am so thankful for my training at the College of Mental Health Counselling.

Janine G., Vancouver, British Columbia

Thank you for the Studies that you have instituted that brought me an education that I have used to further my career in counselling and in life.

Studying my copy of the course text - **can't say enough of how well written and easy learning because of how you wrote it. It's the foundation of my counselling skills.**

Diane Y., Victoria, British Columbia

The content was thorough and helpful, and I have a **greater understanding of the counselling process**. The text was clear and understandable, and it did provide useful skills. I would **recommend the course** for the content.

Robert B., Mount Pearl, Newfoundland

The course has given me some **valuable skills** for what I do. I gained better understanding of counseling grief and awesome techniques for problem solving. Both have already benefitted me.

I have been helping people for some time and completing this course text has given me **skills and a broader knowledge** of how I can incorporate it into my own work. Whether it was resolving conflict, grief counseling, problem solving to name a few this course has given me an edge.

The text was well written making things really clear and understandable. The **skills and techniques are valuable and are already helping me** in what I do.

This course has given me **the exact skills I was looking for** to further better myself at helping mentally ill people put their lives back together. Helping them **resolve conflict and grieve and let go** is much easier and I have **already helped couples with the problem solving techniques**.

I would **recommend this course to others becoming professional counselors** because this **course offers the counseling process in a practical way**. It covers the main concepts in an understanding and effective way. The course is **a wealth of knowledge** to be taken and used.

I have been **applying the skills from this course as I was learning them**. It has given me an even better edge on the work I do, and I'm very thankful I have had the opportunity to do the course.

Melissa T., Nova Scotia

The course was **more complete than I had expected for the cost** of tuition. Having **many example statements** made it easy to understand the different areas in the process of counselling. Although I know that I still have much to learn, and will need to gain a great deal of experience before I become a professional counsellor, I believe this **course has**

given me a solid foundation of the counselling process. I am confident that **I have gained the necessary skills to begin helping people** through counselling.

I also had not expected to **uncover so much about myself**, and my own struggles, and their connection to my family of origin. I welcomed this insight as it is, in a way, finally freeing me. My journey to recovering from my past and present problems has taken a healthy turn as I've recognized, and am **changing my unhealthy behavior patterns, thanks to this course**.

A combination of the knowledge I've acquired into the mental health counselling field and the insight into the background of my own problems is what would propel me to **recommend this course to others** who are interested in becoming professional counsellors.

As I gain some experience through a student intern program, I would also like to further my development as a professional counsellor by studying various subjects, in depth, to specialize in the treatment of mood disorders, anxiety disorders, and psychotic disorders. I would also like to develop skills in cognitive behavioural therapy and life coaching.

Gina S., Nova Scotia

I found that this course **thoroughly touched upon all the counselling skills that a counsellor would need** to begin a counselling career. There was a lot of information, but the more I read the more I understood, and the way the assignments were developed allowed me to go over the information again and again so I could learn it more. This course has **definitely exceeded my expectations**. It has **challenged the way I think about my own life**.

By breaking down the **counselling process step by step it has made it easy to process the information** and to see how it applies to everyone. The course didn't only explain the process but took me through the most **common emotional problems and demonstrated a pattern for dealing with each** one so that anyone with a problem can be helped. Not only were the major personality disorders discussed but also the **basic problems of everyday people and everyday life**.

The **text was very easy to understand**. The skills were demonstrated in such a simple manner that it sounded like common sense. I feel like I could talk to anyone now and give them some sort of positive useful information, not only about major life trauma but about simple, everyday problems.

Not only would I recommend this course to others who want to be counsellors, **I would recommend it to anyone who is in any kind of helping position**. This course has given me an understanding of how emotions work and how to deal with them. It has also taught me things about myself that I never realized and how to communicate better. This course would be beneficial to everyone and would **give everyone stepping stones for dealing with life's problems**, big and small.

Gail M., MSW, St. Petersburg, Florida

In my sincere opinion I **received value in counselling skills and knowledge exceeding the cost of tuition** for this course.

Thank you for offering me this experience to take stock of my practice and add new understanding to the work I do. The course provides a workable schema to flow from present to past, to relate current dysfunctional behaviour and faulty belief systems to the original source.

William H., professional counsellor, San Diego, California

I must say that I am truly **honored and impressed by your genuine humble way to share such valuable clinical information** for all to use. I have read most of your work and have used them in my counseling. I just wanted you to know that I appreciate you and your work. Thank you.

Nicki K., Melbourne, Australia

The course was **very thorough and very interesting**. I immensely enjoyed reading the text book and its in-depth discussions of how to conduct a counselling session, the things to look for and what to say. It definitely **went beyond my expectations** because I was thinking the course would only involve a theoretical view of counselling. Instead it was **quite hands-on with many great practical examples**.

I definitely think the knowledge and skills I learned in this course have given me a **solid foundation for counselling** my future clients. Beginning with a clinical assessment is a great way to build a counselling relationship and something that I think is unique to the author of the text book, and is definitely a beneficial skill I have learned.

I **understand now that one must be gentle with people when they are recounting their childhood** and relationship issues. I have also learned an important lesson about how to use limited time effectively and how to encourage someone to talk about their most private and difficult issues without scaring them away.

These skills if perfected with repeated practice, will allow me to become a counsellor who clients will want to talk to, even about their most difficult issues. I know this is an important skill to have because being able to encourage a person to link the past with the present is key in aiding clients become healthier and happier people.

Similarly it was **extremely useful to learn exactly what to say in some of the more difficult situations** clients may discuss, and I definitely feel ready to begin to help people.

With regards to the wording of the text, I think it was written very well. All the **explanations were simple and easy to understand** which was great. In terms of providing me with the essential skills for becoming a successful counsellor, I think it did provide **many practical skills especially with ways to help the sessions** begin, progress and close. However I think it would have also been useful to have been provided some more information about how to characterise disorders and how to specifically deal with them (which will come in later individual subject courses).

I would like to learn how to characterize and work with client's with different disorders. I will also need to learn, through practice, how to be careful yet effective when dealing with particularly painful issues. I will probably also have to work on my listening skills.

I would **recommend this course to others because of its practical approach to delivering great knowledge and tips on how to be an effective counsellor**. The text is clear, simple to understand, and very informative about how to begin your counselling career. I just wanted to thank the author very much for writing this course and giving me the wonderful opportunity to learn what it takes to be a counsellor.

Fred Lee, Hong Kong, China

Wonderful, the course **provides the critical knowledge, skills, and attitude to be a counsellor**; the knowledge and skills I learned in the course have given me a solid foundation for counselling people who are seeking help.

Not only **develop a strong and solid foundation for counselling** people, but also provide the **significant and systematic process**, document, and operational practices, together with the professional code of conduct and ethics.

Appreciate the **text is very useful and of high value to someone who wants to become a successful professional counsellor**.

Such a **comprehensive knowledge, skills, and experiences will be beneficial to my development as a professional counsellor**. It is really **an excellent course** for someone to be a professional counsellor in the future.

Absolutely **recommend not only to my friends, associates, and networks, but also want to contribute more by working close and collaborating with Daniel to provide the course in Hong Kong**.

Daniel is a very experienced and professional counsellor. With his guidance, training materials, mode of assignments, and examination, in my opinion, **I received the value and counselling skills and knowledge exceeding the cost of tuition** for this course.

Last but not the least; I sincerely thank you very much for the **continuous guidance, support and assistance** from Daniel who helps me complete this course.

William M., Thailand

The course **exceeded my expectations**. It is **applicable and relevant** to the real world. I would **definitely recommend this course to anyone** who is interested in counselling.

The course has provided me with a solid backbone of knowledge for counseling and helping others. It is a **great source of information and can always be referred to** at any time. The knowledge and skills gained from this book **give me the confidence to know the right questions to ask**, when to act, and when not too.

The course text is in an easy-to-read form. It **takes the reader from a basic ground level of understanding to a solid foundation** to counsel others. Each chapter of the book flows into the next, making it easy to read.

I would **recommend this course to others because of the immense amount of knowledge** that one gains after completing this course. The price is good, and what you learn is definitely worth the money.

In my sincere opinion, this **course was excellent for the cost**. I feel that some people that go to university for four years, do not have the same knowledge that someone has after taking this course. Thank you.

Wendy J., Trinidad

In my view the value I've received in terms of self-confidence, self-efficacy, personal healing and growth, and professional preparedness, far exceeds what I have paid for tuition.

I would **recommend this course without hesitation** because I believe that the content is more than enough to prepare anyone with appropriate skills for an efficient and effective counselling practice. The code of ethics, the detailed techniques, and the specifics on guidelines, principles and approaches are presented in a clear, simple, and direct way that almost anyone would feel motivated to excel in the helping profession.

I expected this course to give me effective skills for counselling. I have **received much, much, much more in terms of the personal challenges** I had to embrace, the insights into the residual dynamic of conflicts and losses and their effects on my current relationships and my ability to perform on a personal as well as on a professional level.

I believe that self-knowledge is a critical and powerful tool that equips a person to "walk in another person's shoes." This **course has re-introduced me to myself on a very deep level** and so as I have been able to identify my core issues and attempt to address them. I know that I am now able to apply the knowledge and skills to be effective in counselling others who seek help.

The **text was indeed written in a clear, understandable style**. In fact the style was quite **conversational and I felt like I was actually participating in real-time live class** discussions. The skills provided are extremely useful and essential, and the content is presented in such clear detail that the layperson can truly feel confident to offer herself to journey with others through the counselling process to mental health. This text is indeed **serving to democratize essential counselling skills, not only for professional practice but also for personal growth and development**.

Wendy A., Port of Spain, Trinidad

The course **more than met my expectations** because I gained so much knowledge. I was made more aware of myself, how I function and why I function as I do – family of origin. This was really rigorous and very, very deep. I gleaned more skills as well, which I impart to my students and to clients in my private practice.

Having done this course, I feel more confident. I am able to discuss areas in counselling comfortably. My skills have been sharpened and I can now use them when I see clients, when I lecture and when I talk to other counsellors and psychologists. I am proud of myself because my foundation has been strengthened. I gained so much in skills, knowledge, interventions. I can walk, talk and work more confidently now that I have gained so much more knowledge.

The **text was quite clear and the language and expressions were very down to earth**. I loved the examples used, these were very real and practical ones. Some of them I encounter and I am able to make more sense of them now. I felt as though I was in session or invited by you to sit in on a counselling session. The text which was well written. **Information on all aspects of counselling were included**. It provided me with **"hands-on" experience and 'know-how' in carrying on a counselling session**. I plan to use the **text as my "Bible."**

I am particularly enamoured with the **Clinical Assessment which I have begun using, and the various interventions** presented for all psychopathologies. I am grateful for these. The text encapsulated the goals of counselling and the skills necessary to carry on the processes.

I wish to become proficient in carrying out the Enactment technique and using the Empty Chair technique. I want to know how to do everything with counselling correctly, practically, to give appropriate treatment to my clients, and **to read this text over and over and over to become very well grounded** and respected in this field.

I would **recommend this course to some of my students who are interested in becoming professional counsellors** because I know they have the potential and personalities suited to this profession. They are very keen, they have the skills required of counsellors which are genuineness, they are open-minded, they show empathy, and unconditional positive regard, they are reflective thinkers, they are mature and they are warm individuals who would put their shoulders to the wheel in their approach to this course, which requires total commitment as it is extremely rigorous.

I have **certainly received value in counselling skills and knowledge that far outweighs the cost of tuition for this course**. The examples presented in the text are so practical that I can relate to them and learn very well from them. I feel more confident that my body of knowledge has increased, now that I have been exposed to the literature presented in the course content. My counselling skills have improved because I have seen how they have been used in the many cases presented in the text. **Everything makes more sense to me now**. What I learned in the classroom has now come to light.

P.N., Pune, India

The course is **very comprehensive and gives a good overall view of the counseling** sessions, their framework, what needs to be done, how to conduct it. Another thing I liked very much were the counselor responses that are to be given at every moment with the client.

The text provided me with **useful practical skills that will enhance my practice**. I would **recommend this course to others who are interested in becoming professional counsellors**, because it provides a nice foundation to build on.

Bernice E., Nigeria

The course met my innermost desire on counseling psychology. It helped me to know **how to handle some situation even for myself and other people** as a whole. I now see why people behave the way they do. I desire now to help as many as possible who may be needing my help. I found the **text very useful, very important** and broadens ones knowledge in some situations.

I **recommend this course** to others because it's a **must-have training** in awareness of oneself and others.

I received value in counselling skills and knowledge exceeding the cost of tuition for this course because **knowledge when acquired pays more than the amount spent to acquire it**; in the future it helps many situations.

Edna F., Weyburn, Saskatchewan

This course exceeded my expectations on what I believed I would benefit from it. It was very specific and easy to follow. Through repetition of the process and the course lay out, it gave me the knowledge and confidence in knowing the information. I have gained **insight into both my personal and professional journeys**.

The knowledge and skills I learned in the course have given me a **solid foundation for counselling people** who are seeking help. It taught me how to facilitate a therapeutic relationship with clients, how to engage them in their journey of healing and self-actualization. It taught me specific ways to help people reach into what makes them tick. It was also extremely helpful in teaching me **what is and is not effective** and appropriate in the counselling process.

The text in this course was **written in a clear, understandable** way. It provided useful, essential skills and details for becoming a successful professional counsellor. I especially found the examples very useful. I found that this course paid close attention to detail when describing how the process works.

I would **recommend this course to others** who are interested as it gives one a comprehensive understanding and knowledge of the counselling process **from beginning to end**.

I would say that I have received value in this course. I don't believe that I can put a monetary value on the knowledge I have gained. Therefore the **value exceeds the cost of tuition**.

Linda C., Saskatchewan

This course did exceed my expectations. The volume and level of learning work was **far beyond what I had experienced in any classes**. The value gained was that through the extensive work load a vast and secure knowledge of the converse content was for sure gained. I feel comfortable now to use the tools presented in this book in my counselling work, as they have been very clearly explained. This knowledge has given me a **more confident approach** to therapy.

I feel my level of expertise has been greatly increased from this course. The **knowledge was both theoretical and practical and therefore user friendly for myself**. One practical example would be the empty chair technique. I had heard of it before but now more fully understand how to use and implement it into my work.

The **text is self is a very useful and well written tool**. It will be a tool that I will keep close at hand in my practise, because I know that I will refer to it after. The clarity and detail with which things are explained is very useful indeed. The **practicality of the approaches in this book made it an easy read** and provided a good grasp of general knowledge in the area of counselling. I did find the level of work expected to complete the exam very intensive. I did learn a tremendous amount about the book however through the process.

I will continue to study and learn new tools as I find the area of counselling an ever changing place. We always have new clients with new issues to present. I am an avid reader and learn a lot that way. I also like to take courses and workshops. I am getting more comfortable at making my way around the internet and it's many many resources. I found the info on pages 288 to 308 very valuable.

I would **recommend this course to others** but I would encourage them to enter into with the understanding that it is a **tremendous amount of work**. The reward and learning have been great as well but knowing ahead of time about the workload would have helped me.

There is **no question that I did receive valuable learning** from taking this course. I **have used some of the tools already and will continue to do so**. I found **the personal work that came along with this course very useful**.

Judy M., Scarborough, Ontario

The course helped me to get **the foundation I needed** for counselling; a very "hands on" or "how to do it"course with **lots of examples** from real life. It **helped me to gain more confidence** and feel that "I can do it." The text is clear and concise. It gives **all the necessary tools needed** to be able to go through a counseling session with a client

I want to build on this foundation combined with practical experience in order to be able help people address their issues and find long lasting solutions to improve the quality of their lives.

I would **definitely recommend** it because it is very well structured and guides you step by step through the entire process.

The course is definitely a needed tool and **met my expectations**. Comparing with the prices on the market, I would say the price is competitive.

Hiidoon M., Houston, Texas

When I signed up for the course I had no idea it would be so intense and demanding. The course **content is very rich and covers almost every area that was lacking in the social work program I attended**. All my questions about the counseling relationship have been thoroughly addressed. The **practical guide** concerning the actual counseling session, what to say at the opening of the session, to generate insight, closing, even how to make a phone call are invaluable and will form a good reference tool for me in practice.

The text was written in a clear understandable way, and it did provide useful skills that I will rely on until I become comfortable with counselling and develop my own style.

I would primarily **recommend the course because it is 100% online** which works well for busy professionals. The **cost is also reasonable considering the huge amount of knowledge you acquire** which higher paying educational institutions cannot offer. I definitely know this course gave me more value in counselling skills and knowledge than the cost of tuition.

Reginald B., Minneapolis

This course exceeded my expectations in that the **fees were reasonable** for someone struggling financially. The time allotted for course completion is reasonable and extensions are granted if needed. The book for the course is an easy read even for a novice. The **book content is applicable to real world situations and far exceeds** what is taught in the college classroom.

I took the course because the staff that I work with are not prepared to be professional counsellors as evidenced by my observations and listening to them. I knew that I needed to develop the skills necessary to effective with clients. **Since taking this course, my participation in weekly supervision has increased exponentially**. I use it during group work and my **co-facilitators are amazed** at how I facilitate.

Absolutely without a doubt I received value in counselling skills and knowledge exceeding the cost of tuition for this course! I need to further study the book to understand more.

Virginia T., California

I learned a lot of **valuable insight to working with mental illness** and how to handle a crisis. I have been able to polish my skills and obtained valuable information that will **assist me in treating my clients**. The text was very informative, I **learned a lot of clinical terms that I face every** day but had no knowledge that there was a name for the behaviors that my clients display. I would **definitely recommend this course** to anyone who wants to gain insight and knowledge in mental health counseling. The outline of the course **met all my expectations** and is **worth the cost of the tuition**.

Connie S., British Columbia

I found the course to be **helpful in understanding myself** and feel that it could also **help me to start my career in counseling**.

The knowledge and skills I learned in the course have given me a **solid foundation for counseling people** who are seeking help because I now have an **understanding of different behaviours and disorders**, and understand **why people are the way they are** and how I can help them.

I would **recommend this course to others** as it is **full of helpful information** for someone who wants to **start a career in counseling**.

Natalie B., Nova Scotia

This course was **very helpful in refreshing, enhancing and adding to my knowledge of counseling skills**, practices and protocols. I was pleasantly **surprized at the amount of knowledge** involved with this course of study, the information was **well laid out and the assignment was very effective in creating a learning** environment outside of a classroom. The program advisor was very supportive when I needed extensions and for that I am thankful. I felt able to approach him at any time. The **text book was easy to follow and the information it contained was extensive, useful and relevant particularly the dialogue demonstrations** and the appendixes that were included. I feel better equipped to work with helping others because of this program.

The knowledge and skills within the program have **enhanced my working knowledge** from previous education (Counseling diploma, Certified Nursing Assistant, BA of Community Studies, and Masters of Ad.Ed) and my work experiences with high risk families with Public

Health Services. I've **learned many new concepts that add to the foundation I had such as the enactment exercise**, the added knowledge of **specific disorders** and the protocols for situations such as **suicide and homicide**. The **dialogue demonstrations have helped me with the dialogues I have with my families when they are in crisis or seeking change** in unhealthy behaviors in themselves and/or their children.

The knowledge in this program has made me **feel more confident in my skills**; it has solidified my desire to **continue my quest for a career as a counselor** possibly in my own practice.

The **text book was well written and well organized.** I appreciated **the flow of the skills and practices** and how they were presented. This made it **easy to follow and stay on track with the amount of skills being taught** as well as with the initial assignment requiring clear, researched answers. The **text has been a wonderful resource and I plan to keep it with me when I am working as a reference tool**. The **dialogue samples are very realistic** and that makes them very helpful when working with various people experiencing various situations.

I will be looking forward to doing supervised practical work with a licensed counselor in order to get the understanding of what it's like in a practice and working with a variety of clients in a mental health capacity. I still have lots to learn and am looking forward to doing so. I would like to gather more knowledge regarding specific disorders and ways to best support people living with them, as well as a working knowledge of the DSM. I also look forward to attaining some business skills in the event that I do get the opportunity to open a practise when I have completed my career with Public Health. I will take any learning opportunity made available to me regarding counseling and skill enhancement. I am attending a motivational interviewing refresher course soon and I am very excited about that.

I would **recommend this program to others** and I have, because it is **accessible, informative, realistic, interesting and affirming for those who have had educational and work experience in the field of**

counseling. This program **challenges your thinking regarding counseling practices** and helps establish an **understanding of boundaries**, the reasons we have them and how to stay within them. I think this program can support the person embarking on a new career journey and encourage them to seek as much knowledge to support them in doing so.

The **skills and knowledge I have obtained in this program has certainly exceeded the cost of tuition**. I am a strong proponent for online and correspondence learning and I believe **the program challenged me and offered me similar learning experiences** that a more expensive program would have offered. I am exceedingly grateful I found this program as I have exhausted my educational financial resources with **my master's degree completed last year**, but felt like I needed this piece to complete the puzzle of my goal of being a counselor and being recognised as such. I do the work; I study the skills and knowledge and need to reaffirm my level of certification to increase my eligibility in the field. I feel **the course will allow me to do all of this at a cost that is incredibly affordable**.

Thank you for this **wonderful learning experience** and opportunity.

Donna W., Alberta

The Mental Health Counsellor Training Course has definitely met my expectations. By doing this course I have been **able to implement the tools that I have learned and been more effective in my job**. I also became more **aware of how I can approach my clients in a more therapeutic way**.

I have found that **by using the assessment it helps me to see where the client is and what they have been through in their life**. I have been given the **knowledge and skills that make me more effective in counselling people**. Currently I work in a Domestic Violence Centre and **now am able to give my clients an assessment** that they clearly are in control of when it comes to what they need to work on. I also have the **skill to recognize how I need to approach very delicate situations**.

The test was written in a clear and understandable way. I found that it **provides useful, essential skills and details for becoming a successful professional counsellor**. By doing this test I have learned to think outside the box and have a deeper thought pattern.

I would **recommend this course to others who are interested in becoming professional counsellors**, because I have **learned an amazing amount of skills that I can use** in my profession. Also I **feel more confident** with the knowledge that I have acquired doing this training. Also it is nice to have the **flexibility of being able to do this training on my own time** and being able to get extensions granted when needed.

I feel that my counselling skills are better now, since I have learned another different way to approach the issues at hand. I really **enjoyed this training** and value it a lot and am excited to pursue my career. I feel that what the training cost me is very beneficial and for **what I have learned has exceeded the cost of the tuition**. Thank you for the opportunity to have taken this course online!

Cynthia M., Yukon

The course definitely went beyond my expectations because I was thinking the course would only involve a theoretical view of counselling. Instead it **was quite hands on with many great practical examples**. The knowledge and skills I learned in this course have given me **a solid foundation for counselling my future clients**.

Beginning with a **clinical assessment is a great way to build a counselling relationship**, and is definitely a beneficial skill I have learned. I understand now that you **must be gentle with people** when they are recounting their childhood and relationship issues. I have also learned an important lesson about how to use limited time effectively and how to encourage someone to talk about their most private and difficult issues without scaring them away. Having **these skills will allow me to become a counsellor who clients will want to talk to**, even about their most difficult issues.

With regards to the wording of the text, I think it was written very well. **All the explanations were simple and easy to understand** which was great. In terms of providing me with the essential skills for becoming a successful counsellor, I think it did provide many practical skills especially with **ways to help the sessions begin, progress and close.**

Having a full time job and a household to run it was great to be able to study when time was available The text is **clear, simple to understand, and very informative** about how to begin your counselling career

This course have given me a solid foundation for counselling my future clients. I just want to thank the Daniel Keeran very much for writing this book and giving me **the wonderful opportunity to learn what it takes to be a counsellor.**

Frances B., NWT, Canada

I was excited to take the course but I was not sure that an online course would be able to teach me the skills to feel confident in saying I know how to conduct a counselling session. **I was VERY wrong.** From very early on I realised this course was **far more in depth than I had imagined** possible.

The skills I've learned in the course have given me the confidence to know what to say in many if not most conceivable situations. I know now that **everything you say in a counselling session is very precise and deliberate.**

Yes, the **text was in casual and easy to read language** which helped me to really engage with the text.

I **currently work as a social worker** and so I am lucky enough to **already be able to put the skills learnt in this course to very good use** but in the future I plan to read A LOT more about counselling and techniques with a view to making a move into more professional counselling.

I would recommend the course for the reasons given above, and I thought the **cost of the course was worth the expense!**

To Register, simply complete the Registration Form at
www.collegemhc.com The course text, materials, and
assignments will be emailed immediately with a hard copy of the
text sent by regular mail. Time extensions for completion are
approved on request.

www.ingramcontent.com/pod-product-compliance
Lightning Source LLC
Chambersburg PA
CBHW060650290526
45793CB00001B/482